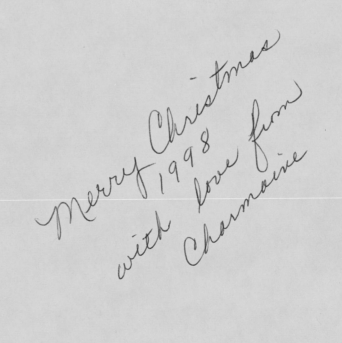

Merry Christmas
1998
with love from
Charmaine

ST.CHARLES

—— MISSOURI ——

Photography by Gene Howard,
Sue Vanderbilt, and Peggy Bradbury

Compiled by Bob McElwee

Phoenix Publishing

Manufactured in the United States of America.
Printed on acid-free paper.

Library of Congress Cataloging-in-Publication Data
McElwee, Bob.
    St. Charles : Missouri / photographs by Gene Howard,
    Sue Vanderbilt, Peggy Bradbury.
    ISBN 1-886154-00-7

Design by Grace Delcano

Phoenix Publishing
300 West Main Street
Urbana, Illinois 61801

On reverse: Photography by Gene Howard

GH

INTRODUCTION

St. Charles, Missouri, was settled in 1769 by Louis Blanchette, a French Canadian hunter and fur trader. Since then, the city of St. Charles has grown with the country, establishing its own unique and dynamic history. St. Charles has been vital to United States history because of its central-ized geography and its waterways, as well as the people who have made this unique town their home. The timeline beginning on page 6 gives a taste of this past, and covers more than 225 years.

This book is meant to highlight, through pictorial representation, some of this historic past as well as present-day St. Charles and its surrounding area. If you have ever walked on Main Street and down to the depot perhaps you may recall the distinct aroma of aging wood in the antique stores, the taste of old-fashioned ice cream from the soda shop, or the feeling of a warm gentle breeze on your face while sitting in the gazebo in the park. Re-explore the unique restored homes and shops, as well as the festivals and other entertainment of this historic site.

CONTINUED ▶

The images in this book are a collection of actual archive photographs, hand-tinted photographs of present-day St. Charles, and current color photographs by four midwestern photographers. It will give you a hint of the magnificence of the architecture, the breathtaking beauty of the countryside and the dramatic riverboats of the area, as well as St. Charles' unique position in rail and river transport.

The first time I came to St. Charles was during a vacation with my family. Besides being a photographer's dream location, I remember I was most impressed with the care that had been taken to preserve the buildings and the area. Later, I learned this was not by accident—countless organizations and individuals with the insight to realize the great value of St. Charles' heritage had worked hard to preserve it. The result is a destination that evokes a feeling of an earlier century when the history of our country was still evolving.

Early one morning I was taking a photograph of Main Street. I could almost hear the drum and fife, and the sound of soldiers marching in step, as well as the steam locomotive of yesteryear passing along the trestle. Let this book guide you on an imaginary journey through the streets and countryside of St. Charles and experience the charm and beauty of this historic community.

Bob McElwee

ST.CHARLES

ST. CHARLES THROUGH TIME

This timeline provides some historic highlights of this incredible city and its surrounding area. To give a sense of the time periods and a feeling for the city itself, reproductions of actual historic photographs are included. In addition, contemporary photographs by St. Charles writer and photographer Peggy Bradbury are included, featuring reconstructed historic scenes enhanced by her unique hand-tinting technique. Archival photographs are provided courtesy of the St. Charles Historical Society.

Population of St. Charles, according to census, is 225.

1762

By secret Treaty of Fontainebleau (Nov. '62) Louis XV ceded all Louisiana west of the Mississippi River, plus New Orleans to Carlos III of Spain.

1769

Louis "Le Chasseur" Blanchette, a French-Canadian, settles in St. Charles with his wife and friends. The trading post/settlement is called Les Petites Côtes, or Little Hills. Blanchette erects a grist mill on the bank of Blanchette Creek.

1791

The settlement officially changes its name to San Carlos, to honor both Charles IV of Spain and San Carlos Borromeo, the patron saint of the new Catholic Church.

Improvement Association Parade
Main Street. St. Charles. Mo.

1797

The first school in St. Charles, a French Catholic school, opens to tutor young ladies.

1799

Daniel Boone settles in St. Charles County with his wife and family on land granted to him by the government of Spain.

1800

Daniel Boone is appointed "syndic," or county judge, of the Femme Osage District in St. Charles County. Boone holds court under a huge old elm tree on his property that becomes known as the "Judgement Tree."

1802

The Millington brothers (Seth and Jeremiah) plant their first castor bean seeds to produce their own castor oil. They are so successful that St. Charles lays claim to being the castor oil capitol of the world, until a cholera epidemic in 1833-1834 fells the two brothers and many townspeople.

1803

Napoleon takes control of Spanish-owned lands from the Mississippi to the Pacific Ocean. He deeds the land to the United States government for $15,000,000 (4 cents per acre). The so-called Louisiana Purchase doubled the size of the country.

In May, Lt. William Clark and his frontiersmen leave their winter camp near Wood River, Illinois, and dock in St. Charles. There, they pick up Meriwether Lewis, who arrives overland from St. Louis. On May 21, the *Corps of Discovery* sets up the flood-swollen Missouri River, seeking the way to the Pacific Ocean.

The population of St. Charles is 850 which includes 55 slaves.

After two years, the Lewis and Clark Expedition returns, passing through St. Charles on its way to St. Louis, the journey's end.

1804

Lt. William Clark observes in his journal that St. Charles "...is composed of nearly 100 small wooden houses, besides a chapel. The inhabitants, about 450 in number, are chiefly descendants of the French of Canada. In their manner they invite all the careless gaiety and amiable hospitality of the best times of France."

1805

Aaron Burr, third Vice President of the United States, later convicted of treason, comes to St. Charles to confer with Revolutionary War veteran Timothy Kibby.

1806

General Zebulon Pike sets out from St. Charles on an expedition to explore the western and southwestern part of the Louisiana Purchase.

St. Charles Post Office is established on August 1 and is the third post office to be established west of the Mississippi.

1809

St. Charles is incorporated as a city.

1815

Peace Treaty between the U.S. Government and the Indian Confederation, headed by Tecumseh, is signed at Portage des Sioux. The treaty ended the Indian hostilities begun during the War of 1812.

The Missourian, published by Robert McLoud, becomes the town's first newspaper.

St. Charles serves as the first capitol of the new state of Missouri.

1818

The founder of Chicago, Jean Baptiste Pointe du Sable, dies and is buried in Borromeo Cemetery. Du Sable, the offspring of mixed ethnic heritage— his father was a white French-Canadian and his mother was a black Haitian—married a Potowatami Indian. They had a daughter, Suzanne, and a son, Jean. Du Sable spent the last ten years of his life in St. Charles with his son and granddaughter, no longer socially accepted by the increasingly white, Americanized city he had founded.

1819

The steamboat *Independence* proves that the Missouri River is navigable.

1820

Daniel Boone dies and is buried beside his wife, Rebecca, on Femme Osage Creek near Marthasville, Missouri.

Boone's Lick Road opens. The 150-mile trail leads to a salt lick owned by Daniel Boone and his sons. Later, the road marks the first leg of the Santa Fe and Oregon Trails.

1821-1826

Published by the Chamber of Commerce, *The Progressive St. Charles—1916* included this commentary: "The 43 legislators presented quite a contrast. Many were well-educated and well-mannered; however, some were rough characters. Most dressed in homespun clothes, buckskin leggings and hunting shirts, and home-made shoes or moccasins. Most wore hats of skins of wild cats or raccoons."

Sue Schneider in *Old St. Charles* quotes one representative as commenting: "I am no book larnt man, but there is a few who can beat me swapping horses or guessing the weight of a bar [of iron]. I come here because my people voted for me, knowing I was an honest man and could make as good whiskey and apple brandy at my still as any man."

1822

The first public school in St. Charles opens at 131 Jefferson Street.

The first wave of German
immigrants come to the
Missouri Valley.

1827

Lindenwood College for
women is established by
George and Mary Sibley.
It later comes to be
known at the "Wellesley
of the West."

Ten years later, in 1837,
Sibley assists abolitionist
Elijah Lovejoy in escaping
a mob following an anti-
slavery sermon.

1838

The annual city expenses
are listed as $848.56.

1839

St. Charles College opens
at 117 North Third Street.
During the Civil War,
the college houses
Confederate prisoners.
Later still, Rupert Hughes
and his brother, Howard
Hughes Sr. (father of the
tycoon) attend school in
these buildings.

1845

The state of Kentucky
seeks to have Boone and
his wife disintered for re-
burial in Kentucky. Later,
Boone's slave, Alonzo
Callaway, confesses on
his deathbed that he
pointed out the grave of
a stranger when asked to
show the Kentuckians
where Boone was buried.
Mrs. Boone's body was
taken back to Kentucky,
but Daniel Boone still lies
in Missouri. [No matter
what Kentucky may say!]

1850

Rebecca Younger, wife
of outlaw Cole Younger,
dies of birth fever on a
river boat. She is buried
in the Borromeo
Cemetery in St. Charles.

1856

The first train locomotive arrives in St. Charles. Freight and passengers who must cross the river unload on one side, boat to the opposite shore and reload on a new train. From 1864 to 1871, train cars themselves are ferried across the Missouri to and from St. Charles.

1865

The term "soda pop" enters the English language as the result of a patent for a new bottle cap by Zeisler Bottling Co. of St. Charles. When opened, the soda water bottle made a "popping" noise, thus the product became popularly known as "soda pop."

1867

The first public school teacher is hired to teach black children. In 1870, the Franklin School, established for black students, opens at 716 North Third Street.

1871

The longest bridge in the nation, the Wabash Railroad Bridge across the Missouri River at St. Charles, is crossed by its first train.

1873

The St. Charles Manufacturing Co. is organized. Its first order, which is for 50 stock cars, is placed by the St. Louis Iron Mountain and Southern Railway.

1881

The St. Charles Manufacturing Co. becomes the St. Charles Car Company. Under new leadership, the company makes a name for itself by building and designing rolling stock for railroads, helping make the switch from wood to steel-built rail cars. The company also turned out ornate horse-drawn trolleys.

1884

The steamboat *Montana* strikes a pier of the Wabash Railroad Bridge and sinks, but all on board are brought to shore safely. The wreckage resurfaces briefly in 1964.

1886

Playwright Rupert Hughes presents a play at the St. Charles Opera House, 311 North Main Street. His brother, Howard Hughes, has the lead. In earlier times, legend has it, a building on this site disguised a safe haven for slaves on the underground railroad.

1890

The first bridge over the Missouri River opens to pedestrian and wagon traffic. This pontoon bridge was built by Capt. John Enoch, who laid it over 50 barges. The two center barges were moved by cables so that boats could pass through. Unfortunately, ice and rising water caused the bridge to break apart. It is not until 1904 that another passenger bridge spans the Missouri at this juncture.

1893

The Missouri, Kansas and Texas Railroad line, nick-named the "Katy," opens in St. Charles.

Odd-Fellows Hall

On September 5th, the first World War I draftees (all white) bid farewell at the Wabash Depot. The following October, the first contingent of black soldiers departs.

1899

American Car and Foundry (ACF Inc.) purchases the St. Charles Car Company. The company continues to build rail cars and trolleys, including private rail cars for tycoons and hospital cars for the armed forces, over the next half century. Later, during World War II, light tanks built at the plant are test-driven on Main Street. As late as 1994, a train-testing lab owned by ACF Inc. is still in use on the property.

1904

The city's first real highway bridge, the St. Charles Rock Road Toll Bridge, opens to trolley and car traffic just in time for the St. Louis World's Fair.

On August 24 at the fair, Bruce Edwards announced: "We have just spanned the Missouri River...thereby connecting the two richest counties in the state, and making it possible for us to board an electronic car on the streets of our city and alight in the heart of St. Louis within an hour."

1905

"The Marrying Judge," Maxwell P. Frey, opens shop next door to the street car line. Couples ride the streetcar in from St. Louis, walk next door for a brief ceremony, then ride the streetcar out of town. By 1931 Frey claims to have married 8,000 people, a number equal to one third the population of St. Charles.

1915

Hon. William Jennings Bryan, after serving as Secretary of State under Woodrow Wilson from 1913 to 1915, speaks at a "chautauqua," or public tent meeting, in St. Charles.

1917

By this time, the dramatic and musical presentations at the Grand Opera House had given way to motion pictures. In the Spring of this year, the Opera House advertises a showing of "The War's Women," billed as "War's most terrible side, the violation of God's fairest flowers, Women."

The foster son of the last Opera House manager was Frank Culler, a.k.a. Cliff Edwards, who became famous on radio as Ukelele Ike and later was heard as the voice of Jimminy Cricket in the Disney movie "Pinocchio."

St. Charles votes 3,554 to 592 against prohibition.

Over the next several years, the federal government allocates more than half a million dollars for CCC, PNA, and WPA projects in St. Charles County. Projects include construction of flood control dikes, roads, schools, post offices and public swimming pools.

1918

The Missouri Council of Defense declares that henceforth, German should not be spoken in schools, churches or public meetings.

1921

The Grand Opera House closes its doors due to competition from the new electric motion picture houses.

1927

Charles A. Lindbergh, Jr. makes the first solo transatlantic flight, financed by St. Louis businessmen. In earlier days, Lindbergh rode the trolley into St. Charles and drank a quiet beer or two at the Terminal Cafe on North Second Street, recalls James Golden, a supervisor at the nearby American Car and Foundry.

1931

The Missouri 115 (St. Charles Rock Road) highway bridge into St. Charles becomes toll free.

1932

The last streetcar leaves St. Charles on January 18.

Lindenwood College holds its first air raid drill. Students gather in the underground tunnels linking the buildings and wait for the "all clear" before returning to their dormitories.

1935

A runaway passenger coach and several freight cars strike one of the piers supporting the highway (Rock Road) bridge. A section of the bridge falls on North Main Street, injuring five men and smashing two automobiles.

1937

U.S. Route 40 highway bridge opens, connecting St. Louis and St. Charles counties across the Missouri River.

1938

The City Council and Chamber of Commerce sponsor the St. Charles "Pageant of Progress" to boost local morale during the Depression. 15,000 residents participate in four days of activities.

1941

The W.P.A. Guide to 1930s Missouri notes that in St. Charles:

"Progress has scarcely touched the tiny valley, so that the starting point of America's greatest migration has changed little from the time when high-wheeled covered wagons, strings of pack mules and horses, and trudging, impoverished settlers turned hopefully westward along its route."

1942

Gas stations offer to pay a penny for each pound of rubber brought in for the war effort.

Money pours into the city from government contracts, especially for light tanks and other military items made at the American Car and Foundry factory on North Second Street. From 1941 to 1945, the ACF plant in St. Charles provides tanks and hospital cars for the war effort.

The Interstate 70 bridge opens across the Missouri River, just south of downtown St. Charles. This bridge opens the county to developers, making St. Charles one of the fastest growing counties in the nation during the later 1970s and early 1980s.

Missouri's First State Capitol buildings at 208–216 South Main Street, become state historic sites and are restored over the next three years. These rejuvenated buildings become the cornerstone for the South Main Street Historic District and the city's growing tourist trade.

1945

World War II ends on August 15. Of the 1,460 men and 27 women from St. Charles County who joined the military, 47 men were killed during the war.

1954

St. Charles maintained separate schools for black and white students until the fall session of this year.

1957

The Atomic Energy Commission opens the Weldon Spring Plant south of U.S. Highway 40, to process uranium for atomic energy. In the 1940s, TNT is manufactured near the site. In the 1980s, the site becomes infamous for its repositories of chemical and radioactive wastes.

1969

Spurred by a request for $3,000 to restore a house on South Main Street, the city gets a gift of $3,000,000 and Land Clearance for Redevelopment Agency, or "urban renewal," comes to town.

1970

On September 27, the South Main Historic District, an 8-block section of the city dating to 1769, is accepted to the National Register of Historic Places.

The Goldenrod Showboat, built in 1909, is purchased by the city of St. Charles and installed on the riverfront. It is the last working showboat in the United States and was placed on the National Historic Register in 1968.

1990

Disney Studios film *Back to Hannibal* in St. Charles and St. Louis. Since the film was set in pre-civil war times, South Main Street proved an ideal location because the restoration was so accurate and complete. Ned Beatty and Paul Winfield were two of the movie's stars. Jonathan Winters, the comedian, made the round of antique shops in Frenchtown, telling stories.

1991

In March, a large segment of the Frenchtown neighborhood in St. Charles becomes the city's second historic district on the National Register of Historic Places.

1993

St. Charles is one of many counties along the Mississippi and Missouri Rivers hard hit by the great flood of 1993. St. Charles' historic district is spared.

1994

Riverfront Station, a casino boat, opens on the St. Charles riverfront.

The Academy of the Sacred Heart is established in St. Charles by Mother Rose Philippine Duchesne in 1818. In September of that year the Academy opens a free school for poor children which is supported by tuition from the private day school and boarding school.

A woman with a missionary vision, Duchesne could see St. Charles' potential in a global context. She wrote: "Bishop Dubourg, who looks very far into the future, considers this place quite important... American settlers from the eastern states are constantly pouring into this section of the country—restless people who hope St. Charles will become a great commercial link between the United States and China, for the Upper Missouri [River] rises not far from another river that pours its waters into the Pacific Ocean at a place where the crossing to Asia takes just two weeks."

In 1988, Rose Philippine Duchesne, or Mother Duchesne, is canonized, the fourth American to be recognized as a saint by Rome.

St. Charles was not always the picturesque city of restored buildings and quaint shops one sees today. Much of the historic area, has been painstakingly restored, bringing the lively history of this town to life. In the time before the United States broke away from England, this small Missouri city once flew the flags of three countries in a single day!

When the state of Missouri was formed, St. Charles was honored as the capitol city for five years. Serving as a transportation hub, the city was the gateway to the western wilderness. Today, 225 years later, the city still serves as a stopping point, but usually as a traveler's destination.

The brick streets and structures in the restored riverfront area are a reminder of what it was like to be in St. Charles when the country was in its infancy—when gas lights were the only source of illumination in the streets at night, and you could see riverboats rounding the bend in the Missouri River. The boats still run today, but St. Charles now offers its visitors much more than it did in 1769.

According to "Pop" House, owner and proprietor of Pop's General Store on Main Street, the historic restoration effort began during 1965 and continued through the early 1980s until most of the buildings in the district were restored. Today, the Historic District is an open-air museum known worldwide. The number of visitors to St. Charles grows each year, as more and more people discover the beauty and historic significance of this time-honored place.

St. Charles is the oldest city on the Missouri River, a place where history comes alive every day. Walking down its tree-lined streets, stopping to browse in one of its quaint shops, and gazing out onto the water seem to send you back in time, to an age when people spent lazy afternoons on porch swings, watching the boats tug along in the river, feeling a warm breeze fill the Missouri air.

ST. CHARLES TODAY

GH

▲ "Pop" House displays the pioneer memorabilia available in his shop on South Main Street.

GH

An easy walk down Main Street brings you to the Riverfront Station.

St. Charles offers several inviting bed and breakfasts in historic buildings.

BM

SV

▲ A pint-sized, present-day visitor encounters the Revolutionary
War era's Drum and Fife Corps during a reenactment of
Lewis and Clark's 1804 rendezvous and encampment prior to
embarking on their historic expedition.

SV

◀ A fall carriage ride down sunny Main Street enables visitors to enjoy a feeling of the past—when time moved at a slower pace.

▼ Casting a gilded reflection in the waters of the Missouri River, the *Goldenrod Showboat*, built in 1909, is now permanently moored at the south end of Frontier Park. It is once again teeming with life, offering an off-Broadway dinner theater and children's performances.

GH

SV

▲ This old estate has a majestic presence
overlooking its snow-covered yard.

◄ Stained glass captures the afternoon light
in one of St. Charles' many crafts shops.

SV

▲ Winter transforms a familiar vineyard in
nearby Augusta into an impressionistic
landscape.

24

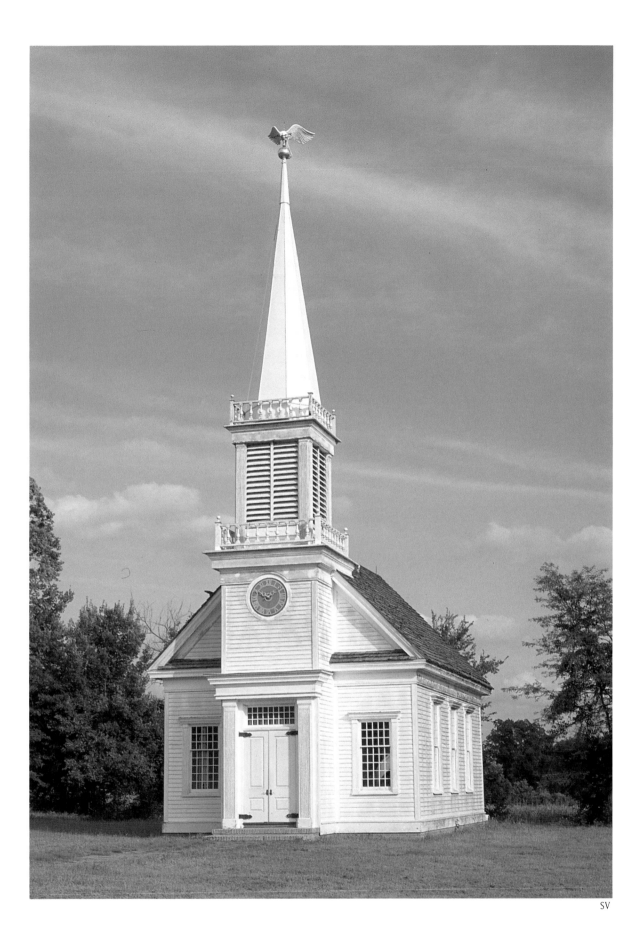

SV

◄ Late evening catches the sparkle of lights in the street-level shop windows of St. Charles' Historic District.

SV

▲ A quiet afternoon in the Peace Chapel reveals patterns of light moving slowly across the pews.

SV

◀ A spinner works by the hearth in the historic home of Daniel Boone in Defiance, Missouri. Construction of the house began in 1803 and was completed in 1810.

▼ Now a museum open year-round, the Daniel Boone Home contains the original Boone family furnishings.

SV

▲ Late autumn turns the grape leaves golden in
nearby Augusta.

GH

GH

▲ Many early settlers arrived in St. Charles by riverboat. Today, visitors can walk aboard replicas of the old, grand paddle wheel-style boats.

▲ The Lewis and Clark Center, located at 701 Riverside Drive, features hands-on exhibits about the famous journey westward.

GH

▲ Varied architectural styles are found in the Historic District of St. Charles — from 1790 French to 1920 American bungalow.

GH

GH

▲ Three modern-day visitors wear the early period costumes of a militiaman, his lady and a washerwoman.

▲ The sun's light dances off stained glass pictures in a shopkeeper's window, giving fantasy and earthly form to the colors of the rainbow.

SV

▲   White winter hills beckon a drive on
St. Charles County's back roads.

BM

◀ This side of Stone Row, built in 1875, faces Main Street. The front faces toward the riverfront.

▼ A contemporary quilt celebrating life is draped outside one of St. Charles' craft shops.

PB

SV

▲   Flint lock "Long Rifles" with powder horns
     were the type used by Daniel Boone. In
     early frontier days, a man's life depended
     on how dry the powder was in his gun.

SV

▲ Couderc Noir grapes and an abandoned
nest sit amid the vineyards of Augusta, only
a short drive from St. Charles.

▲   The brick side of a well-known St. Charles
     bed and breakfast draws the eye upwards.

◄   The bright yellow and purple flowers
     of early spring provide an enchanting
     landscape at Aimee B's Tea Room on
     First Capitol Drive in St. Charles.

GH

◀ Homespun hospitality abounds in St. Charles.

▼ Antiques and treasures are rediscovered daily—this red wagon certainly catches the eye.

SV

▲   These stairs lead up to the Old Courthouse
    of St. Charles.

▲ Fourth-graders learn Missouri history from their "pioneer" teacher.

▲ Transportation through time: the 19th and 20th centuries converge all on one street with horse and buggy, trolley car, and automobiles. Trolley cars officially stopped running long ago, but are a seasonal offering for tourists.

42

SV

▲   Perched high atop the bluffs of Augusta,
Missouri, this summer vineyard overlooks
the Missouri River.

43   ST. CHARLES

SV

▲ Antiques are found throughout the Frenchtown District in St. Charles. Unique for its French-Canadian Colonial architecture dating from 1830 through 1920, this district has been designated as a National Historic District.

SV

▲   Red, white and blue drapes the sky as well
     as the body in this drum corps reenactment
     of the Lewis & Clark Rendezvous in
     St. Charles.

45   ST. CHARLES

GH

◀ Gardeners browse at an outdoor flower market in downtown St. Charles.

▼ Katy Depot, originally built in 1892 to serve the Missouri, Kansas and Texas ("Katy") Railroad, was moved to Frontier Park and restored in 1978.

GH

46

SV

▲   Built in 1769, this historic building was first owned by Louis Blanchette, who
    later sold it to Pierre Chouteau. By 1850, it had acquired its current appearance.
    Originally built to grind grain under water power, the Grist Mill has served
    diverse functions during the past 200-plus years, including producing blankets
    and wool mittens by steam power, as well as operating as both a hospital and
    prison during the Civil War.

SV

▲　Floods have threatened the city several times in
the past but none quite as seriously as the
historic flood of 1993. Fortunately, the Historic
District was spared.

GH

▲   Each year 800,000 people visit the 27 antique
shops, area museums, and walking and biking
trails in and around St. Charles.

▲ Missouri's First State Capitol on South Main Street
has been completely restored and furnished as it
appeared in 1821-26, when the legislature met in
St. Charles. It is open to the public.

50

GH

▶ The Greater St. Charles Convention and Visitors Bureau, built in 1986, was constructed in the style of a hotel that stood on this site from 1822 until the early 1960s.

SV

▲ Candlelight during the winter holidays brightens the dining room at Stake House in Boonesfield Village.

GH

▲   This might be just the right spot for a picnic
lunch in the park.

GH

▲   Early morning in the Historic District is still and
quiet enough to imagine stepping off the curb
into another century.

GH

▲ By late afternoon, a carriage ride can be a welcome rest for tired feet.

◄ In 1990, the film crew for *Back to Hannibal* took advantage of the well-preserved and restored Historic District for their 1850s setting.

GH

BM

▲ Brightly painted doorways and ornate ironwork
   on balconies captivate the eye on a late afternoon walk through St. Charles.

▲ Once standard modes of transportation, steam boats and trolleys now dot the landscape of the city of St. Charles for the enjoyment of visitors.

▶ Fall foliage enfolds the weathered scars of an old barn outside St. Charles.

SV

▲   A winter sun sets on one of the many vineyards in
the picturesque landscape of the St. Charles area.

◀ St. Charles drapes the symbol of both its past and present patriotism from a window of the First State Capitol, built in 1818.

▼ Clothing and travelers' equipment from the early 1800s are on exhibit at the Lewis and Clark Center.

GH

GH

SV

A blacksmith forges a vision of the past for the viewer of the present during the Festival of the Little Hills.

The cobblestone streets of St. Charles provide a quiet respite from the daily commotion of modern living.

GH

SV

▲   Vineyard hillsides offer a panoramic view on a
peaceful summer day.

62

This book designed and produced by
Grace Delcano using PageMaker on a
Macintosh. The type is composed in Matrix.

Compiled by Bob McElwee
Editorial team: Evelyn C. Shapiro,
Pamela Salela, and Sara Hamilton.
Historical Consultant: Gary McKiddy

Jeanette Seamon, Carolyn Whetzel and
Maryan Madden—all guides at the St. Charles
Visitors Center—provided valuable information
for writing the captions.

The St. Charles Historical Society and Greater
St. Charles Convention and Visitors Bureau
offered their support throughout the course
of this project.